CADEL EVANS

CADEL EVANS

THE LONG ROAD TO PARIS

PHOTOS BY GRAHAM WATSON

SBS

hardie grant books

MELBOURNE · LONDON

An SBS book

Published in 2011 by Hardie Grant Books

Hardie Grant Books (Australia)
Ground Floor, Building 1
658 Church Street, Richmond, VIC 3121
www.hardiegrant.com.au

Hardie Grant Books (UK)
Dudley House, North Suite
34–35 Southampton Street, London WC2E 7HF
www.hardiegrant.co.uk

National Library of Australia Cataloguing-in-Publication entry
Evans, Cadel.--
    Cadel Evans / Graham Watson, photographer.
    ISBN: 9781740669863 (hbk.)
    Subjects: Bicycle racing--Pictorial works. Bicycle racing--Popular works.
796.62

Publisher: Pam Brewster
Design: Peter Daniel
Typeset: ITC Lubalin Graph
Colour reproduction: Splitting Image Colour Studio
Printed and bound in China by 1010 Printing International Limited

To Chiara, always

For my fans, my team and cyclists –
and lovers of cycling – everywhere

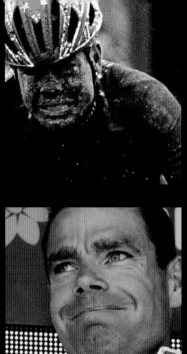

It's been twenty years since I saw my first Tour de France, and in all that time some really good people have believed in me – from my very first coach, Damian Grundy, when I was fourteen years old, right through to my road career.

As everyone is aware, it was Aldo Sassi who really believed in me. He often believed in me more than I did. Aldo said to me last year, 'I'm sure you can win a Grand Tour. I hope for you it is the Tour de France, because that's the biggest and most prestigious tour. If you do that, you will become the most complete rider of your generation'.

He believed in me from October 2001; never for one day did he doubt my abilities. He never gave up on me. I've had some bad moments in the past ten years, but that just makes the good moments even better.

For him to see me now would be quite something.

Introduction

CYCLING IS A SPORT of suffering. When I see Graham's photos, if there's one regular theme I see in the images of me, it's my suffering; but someone once told me, 'For as long as you're willing to suffer, you can be a professional cyclist'. Graham's years of experience have taught him to choose his moments carefully; he takes his photos during the important and decisive moments of a race, when the selection is being made, the winning blows are being dealt, and only the best are out in front: when most of us are suffering.

In modern society we are too cocooned, as human beings, too protected from our environment and our surrounds. Our resistance lowers, our abilities fade – we get too soft. Because of this the fortunate, healthy and wealthy among us need sport: to push our limits, build our strength, maintain our resistance. Sport is something that we need in life. Human character is like a muscle: the more you work it, the stronger it gets. Voluntary suffering, like that we go through in sport, makes a stronger character. Being pushed to the limit we learn to cope; we adapt to resist; we grow stronger physically as well as psychologically.

When we test ourselves on the sporting field, we learn from our mistakes; we improve as human beings while only risking losing a match or a race. It prepares us for life.

1994 – 2008

(FROM LEFT) AT CAIRNS, IN THE AUSTRALIA ROUND OF THE 1994 MOUNTAIN BIKE WORLD CUP; AT MOUNT SNOW, VERMONT, IN THE US ROUND OF THE 1995 MOUNTAIN BIKE WORLD CUP; IN AUSTRALIA, AT THE 1996 SEA OTTER CLASSIC (PHOTOS BY TOM MORAN).

My first attraction to mountain biking was the quiet solitude of being in nature.

I WAS INTRODUCED to cycling through the off-road world of dirt mountain bikes. As well as the appeal of being out in nature, for me, the technical aspects of descending over any terrain, and the lightweight body type required, brought success and encouragement from the early age of fourteen. Still, to this day, those aspects of cross-country racing appeal to me. From a young enthusiastic junior, riding local-level events, to competing in the Atlanta and Sydney Olympics, off-road taught me a lot: training, peaking, being constant throughout a long season, bike-handling skills, concentration, professionalism, working closely with equipment manufacturers, the marketing aspects as well as the possibilities of sport. At the time all of this seemed like merely an in-road to road cycling, but Lance Armstrong was changing the world of road cycling and the 'peculiar' and 'special' aspects of the more 'individual' mountain-bike athlete became the lead in marginal gains and specific preparation for the big races. Was road cycling behind the times? Was mountain biking ahead of its time?

DARIO CIONI, CADEL EVANS, RUNE HOYDAHL AND JEROME CHIOTTI AT SILVES, IN THE PORTUGAL ROUND OF THE 1998 MOUNTAIN BIKE WORLD CUP (PHOTO MALCOLM FEARON/BLISSIMAGES.COM).

THE 1996 OLYMPICS was my first big international event. As a nervous and relatively inexperienced nineteen-year-old I was lucky enough to participate in mountain biking's debut into the Games. This photo captures the concentration that's one of the attributes that helped me achieve successes off-road. Years of specific and meticulous preparation for short but intense races off-road prepared me well for what road cycling is today.

REPRESENTING AUSTRALIA
AT ATLANTA IN 1996.

Early success in mountain biking allowed me the rare opportunity to have a second career in sport.

WEARING THE LEADER'S JERSEY (RED FOR UNDER 23, BLUE FOR ELITE), AT CANMORE, IN THE CANADA ROUND OF THE1998 MOUNTAIN BIKE WORLD CUP (PHOTO BY MALCOLM FEARON/ BLISSIMAGES.COM).

Mountain biking takes you into all conditions and through all terrains.

AT PLYMOUTH, IN THE ENGLAND ROUND OF THE 1998 MOUNTAIN BIKE WORLD CUP (THIS PAGE AND TOP RIGHT), AT NAPA VALLEY, CALIFORNIA, IN THE US ROUND OF THE 1999 MOUNTAIN BIKE WORLD CUP (RIGHT – PHOTOS BY MALCOLM FEARON/BLISSIMAGES.COM).

I first learnt to climb off-road, on the slow
and steep – technical – dirty tracks.

AT PLYMOUTH, IN THE ENGLAND ROUND OF THE 1999 MOUNTAIN BIKE WORLD CUP (LEFT), AND AT NAPA VALLEY, CALIFORNIA, IN THE US
ROUND OF THE 1999 MOUNTAIN BIKE WORLD CUP (RIGHT – PHOTOS BY MALCOLM FEARON/BLISSIMAGES.COM).

Racing off road – while it's not as high profile – to be the best in the world ... it still pushes you to the limit.

COVERED IN MUD AT CANMORE, IN THE CANADA ROUND OF THE 1999 MOUNTAIN BIKE WORLD CUP
(PHOTO BY MALCOLM FEARON/BLISSIMAGES.COM).

AFTER I FINISHED MY career as an Under 23, I took
the opportunity to race with Cannondale's road team
Saeco-Cannondale. I was only competing in smaller
races in between the mountain bike World Cup
events and my performance in both disciplines was
somewhat compromised by the crossover between
the two. The experience, and the opportunities
that the experience opened up in the future, were
compensation for a year when I managed over 30,000
kilometres on the bike, 40,000 kilometres in the car
and 100,000 kilometres in the plane. I was exhausted
by the end of it. But my physique was adapting to the
powerful more-explosive requirements of road racing.
Year by year my muscle mass increased to a heavier,
but stronger and more resistant, level.

ON THE ROAD IN 2000 (ABOVE), AND AT SIERRA NEVADA,
COMPETING IN THE SPAIN ROUND OF THE 2000 MOUNTAIN
BIKE WORLD CUP (RIGHT – PHOTO BY TOM MORAN).

AT THE PARTICULAR moment that I got the jersey, it was a bit surreal. There was so much going on that it was all a little confusing: 'Where am I going? Oh, I'm going to the podium? You want me to stand up there … ? Oh look what I've got! I don't have to wear my Mapei jersey? I've got another one!'

Then, after seven hours of racing in the mountains, when I was already annoyingly running on empty, Noè was upping the pace –

pushing harder and harder to stop any attacks – and I left a bit of a gap. I wouldn't say I was feeling really tired, I was just talking on the radio and lost a little bit of concentration. Hamilton saw the gap and he went on the attack. Then, all of a sudden, bang! My lights went out.

When Hamilton attacked I had to make another surge and that was the very last drop of fuel. I was completely empty.

ON HIS FIRST GRAND TOUR: IN THE 2002 GIRO D'ITALIA (FAR LEFT AND LEFT ABOVE), AND RACING WITH TEAM TELEKOM IN 2003–2004 (ABOVE RIGHT).

THE OPENING WEEK of a Grand Tour is usually quite nervous with all the directors on their radios telling riders to get in this break, or go to the front to avoid that obstacle, and riders taking advantage of their fresh legs to try to make an opportunity for themselves in a break or a sprint. A few hard days soon tire people's nerves, and things calm down a bit.

THE PELOTON DESCENDS ON THE WAY TO MAÇON IN THE TOUR DE FRANCE (LEFT), CLIMBS THROUGH THE ASTURIAS MOUNTAINS ON THE VUELTA A ESPANA (RIGHT TOP AND CENTRE), AND THEN CLIMBS MUR DE HUY IN THE FLECHE WALLONNE (BOTTOM RIGHT).

On the bike, you get a closer perspective on your rivals – how they're riding, how they're pedalling, how fatigued they are, or if they aren't. It's something you have to take into consideration for later in the race, towards the final days.

THE SCENE FROM THE CYCLIST'S SEAT: THE PELOTON ASCENDS COL DU GALIBIER IN THE TOUR DE FRANCE.

THE GIRO DI LOMBARDIA
WINDS ITS WAY ALONG THE
PASSO D'INTELVI.

Going over the Gavia: at 2600 metres, oxygen is a little scarce at almost any speed.

THE BREATH-TAKING PASSO DEL GAVIA, AS THE GIRO D'ITALIA PASSES.

LESSONS LEARNT AS a second-year Tour de France participant ... I was talking to a journalist and asked, 'Don't we leave soon?' The journalist assured me otherwise, and continued with the questioning, even though the race had actually already left. My teammate Chris Horner and I missed the start of one of the longest mountain stages of that year's Tour. Chasing on our own, we rejoined the peloton after about five kilometres, very angry at our stupid and energy-sapping mistake. Chris was sick that day, and ended up losing some twenty minutes to finish in the group of Oscar Pereiro, who would soon be very well known. I was in the final group to the finish, with Levi Leipheimer, Floyd Landis and Denis Menchov. I went hunger flat in the last kilometre, and Menchov rode away from us to win the stage. Years later I am still frustrated by my mistake that day.

CHASING ON STAGE FIVE OF THE
2007 TOUR DE FRANCE.

It's winning that everyone is interested in. Only the victors are remembered

I LOVE MY BIKE, I enjoy racing; I do it a lot but I don't watch much of it on TV. I watch the Tour of Flanders and the Paris–Roubaix every year after my training is complete, and the parts of the Tour that are particularly important, if they're being replayed later while we're having a massage.

STAGE TWENTY OF THE 2007 VUELTA A ESPANA (THIS PAGE), AFTER OVERTAKING DENIS MENCHOV ON STAGE EIGHTEEN (FACING).

I LIKE EVERY ASPECT of cycling, the discipline of work and pushing yourself. Now, as an elite professional, I pay attention to power and heart rate, cadence and training volumes at specific intensities. But when I started I rode because I loved it, and I rode hard because that was better: an opportunity to be by myself, just me and my bike.

Starting riding at two or three years old gave me a base. I wasn't training or anything – it wasn't like I was riding to get better – I just did it because there wasn't anything else.

I have to race whoever turns up. The race decides who is the best. All I have to do is prepare properly and do the best I can.

THE PELOTON, STRUNG OUT THROUGH THE ASTURIAS MOUNTAINS ON THE 2007 VUELTA A ESPANA.

The Ardennes week is something I love. The enthusiasm of all there, and everyone, especially the Belgian fans, coming from Flanders. Being there in the front and in the final – on Mur for Flèche or Sint–Niklaas for Liège – is such a buzz. The atmosphere is incredible.

EMBARKING ON MUR DE HUY IN THE 2008 FLECHE WALLONNE.

Just try ...

... to get to the finish.

Winning: sometimes it comes when you least expect it – like a really pleasant surprise.

CELEBRATING A WELL-EARNED WIN: THE 2008 COPPI E BARTALI.

THE PELOTON SWARMS OVER MONT VENTOUX ON STAGE FOUR (BELOW) AND
CADEL PUSHES THROUGH STAGE FIVE (ABOVE) OF THE 2008 PARIS-NICE.

THE TIME TRIAL (THIS PAGE) AND COMING SECOND ON STAGE
FIVE OF THE 2008 CRITERIUM DU DAUPHINE LIBERE (FACING).

LEADING WITH DENIS MENCHOV ON STAGE TEN OF THE 2008 TOUR DE FRANCE.

Taking yellow on the Hautacam was the first time I'd got the yellow jersey. I think Bernard Hinault was a bit offended when I didn't follow tradition and shake his hand, but I didn't even know the protocols. And after the twenty-four to forty-eight hours I'd just had – nearly crashing out of the Tour, the injury, and then coming back to ride into yellow – it was one of the biggest emotional rollercoasters of my career.

DONNING THE COVETED YELLOW JERSEY AFTER STAGE THIRTEEN OF THE 2008 TOUR DE FRANCE.

RIDING TO YELLOW was a fantastic experience, but defending it with the difficulties I was having with injuries … it ended up being my toughest Tour – far harder than when I broke my arm and finished twenty-sixth in the 2010 Tour de France. It was the most I'd suffered on my bike.

BATTERED AND BRUISED BUT PEDALLING ON THROUGH THE 2008 TOUR DE FRANCE.

THE PELOTON CURVES AROUND COL DE LA LOMBARDE ON
STAGE SIXTEEN OF THE 2008 TOUR DE FRANCE.

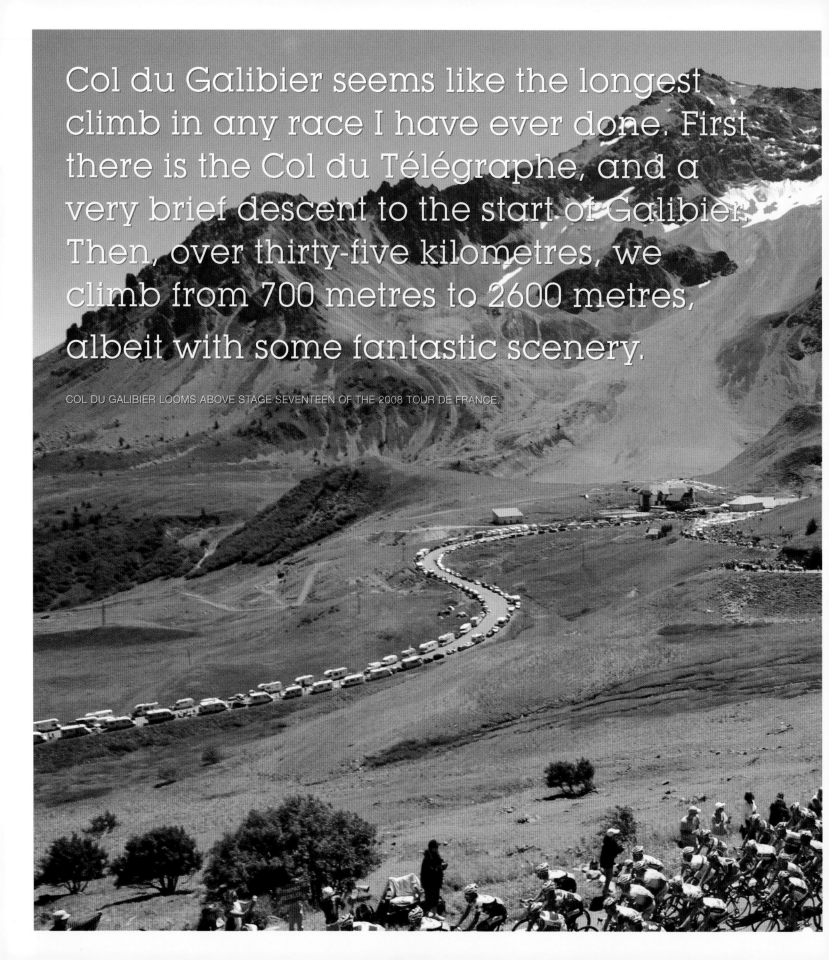

Col du Galibier seems like the longest climb in any race I have ever done. First there is the Col du Télégraphe, and a very brief descent to the start of Galibier. Then, over thirty-five kilometres, we climb from 700 metres to 2600 metres, albeit with some fantastic scenery.

COL DU GALIBIER LOOMS ABOVE STAGE SEVENTEEN OF THE 2008 TOUR DE FRANCE.

Riding up these enormous mountain passes, the peloton looks so lonely and it's so silent up there. When you're riding in a race you've got no time to look at the scenery. You're so concentrated on the race and what's going on around you in the peloton that all these beautiful views just pass you by.

One of the things that's beautiful about cycling is the element of surprise. There are so many variables that it's impossible to predict the outcome.

THE SNOWY PEAKS OF COL DU GALIBIER WATCH OVER THE PELOTON ON STAGE SEVENTEEN OF THE 2008 TOUR DE FRANCE.

LOSING THE TOUR, on the slopes of what is probably the most famous mountain in the cycling world, Alpe d'Huez: the combined efforts of Saxo Banks' Carlos Sastre, Andy and Fränk Schleck put me into a physically and tactically difficult situation. Carlos attacked at the very start of the climb; he took a good gap immediately and continued solidly from there. It quickly isolated most of the GC contenders, but not just from our team. In the chase group a couple of factors came into play: the yellow jersey of Schleck was teammate to Carlos, and his brother Andy was, of course, not going to chase down his own teammate, even if it meant his brother would lose the yellow jersey.

So Carlos, a Spaniard, was out in front. With the Spanish press and public being as informed as they are about cycling and its intricacies, if Alejandro Valverde or Samuel Sánchez were to chase and therefore help me win the tour, they would be crucified by their own supporters. So this left only Bernhard Kohl, Christian Vande Velde and me to chase the lone Sastre out in front. As the best positioned rider and GC I had the most to gain by closing the gap to Carlos, but at the same time I hadn't been at the same level since the heavy crash earlier in the Tour. I was good, but certainly not at my best. If I were to close the gap I would also then have to cover the attacks of the Schleck brothers, one for the stage, the other for the overall, plus the other Spaniards in the race.

A difficult situation. In the end I rode as best I could to limit the time gap to Carlos, while not thinking of the stage result, and leaving enough in reserve to fend off attacks in the final kilometres. Keeping a big enough distance that others wouldn't be able to bridge across it to the leader, but also, with only the time trial to make time back on GC, not so much of a gap that victory would be impossible

Along with the criticism I received from the team for not controlling the situation, it made for a big part of what ended up being the most exhausting Grand Tour I've ever ridden.

THE GRUELLING ALPE D'HUEZ TAKES ITS TOLL IN STAGE SEVENTEEN OF THE 2008 TOUR DE FRANCE.

Over three weeks you experience nearly every aspect of what your body can endure. It's an amazing test of the human physiology. But it's the end that really surprises you. It's amazing to experience how the human body adapts to combat fatigue.

Injuring my knee twelve days before the race didn't give me the best day, physically or mentally.

LEANING INTO A CORNER AT THE 2008 OLYMPIC GAMES.

2009

BEING CONTROLLED BY THE 'SPANISH ARMADA' ON STAGE SEVEN OF THE 2009 CRITERIUM DU DAUPHINE LIBERE.

A DIFFICULT SITUATION on Mont Ventoux: me, with the sprint jersey, against Alejandro Valverde attacking for the win, and Alberto Contador, arguably the best climber in the world. In theory, I only had to cover both of them to defend the jersey into the final time trial. In reality, into a headwind, Valverde – under investigation for his Operación Puerto involvement at the time – attacked early, leaving me to race against Contador, who,

as the better climber with the lesser margin on GC, was the more dangerous rider. He was also rumoured to be in discussions with Valverde's Caisse d'Épargne team – making him effectively a competitor to both of us, but also possibly a teammate to Valverde.

In the end, I rode to close the gap to Valverde with enough in reserve to defend attacks from Contador, who, considering the headwind that day, was in a position to decide who won the Dauphiné Libéré. Valverde took a little more lead than I felt comfortable with, and Contador didn't attack at all ... leaving me to run second again at the Dauphiné for the third year in succession.

IN THE GREEN SPRINT JERSEY ON STAGE SIX OF THE 2009 CRITERIUM DU DAUPHINE LIBERE.

As a rider you have such a different view of the race from what people see on TV – all I've been watching are the four guys in front of me.

THE PELOTON CONFRONTS COL DU LAUTARET IN STAGE SEVEN OF THE 2009 CRITERIUM DU DAUPHINE LIBERE.

REACHING COL DE LA CROIX DE FER ON STAGE SEVEN
OF THE 2009 CRITERIUM DU DAUPHINE LIBERE.

Fear of failure – whether athletes know it

WITH ALEJANDRO VALVERDE ON STAGE NINE OF THE 2009 VUELTA A ESPANA.

or not – is one of the greatest motivators.

IN THE AMARILLO (GOLD) LEADER'S JERSEY TAKING STAGE NINE
OF THE 2009 VUELTA A ESPAÑA WITH ALEJANDRO VALVERDE.

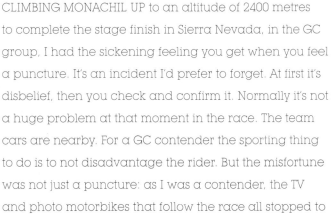

CLIMBING MONACHIL UP to an altitude of 2400 metres to complete the stage finish in Sierra Nevada, in the GC group, I had the sickening feeling you get when you feel a puncture. It's an incident I'd prefer to forget. At first it's disbelief, then you check and confirm it. Normally it's not a huge problem at that moment in the race. The team cars are nearby. For a GC contender the sporting thing to do is to not disadvantage the rider. But the misfortune was not just a puncture: as I was a contender, the TV and photo motorbikes that follow the race all stopped to capture the incident, blocking the road and holding up the team cars, and hence my team assistance.

Along came the Shimano Neutral Support (there to assist everyone, and with no team affiliations); they're in the first cars following the main part of the race. But complications only increased, with confusion over our Campagnolo 11 speed components and gearing, along with a little incompetence on their part. I was flat-out concentrating on staying calm, considering I still had a descent and a twenty-kilometre climb up to a 2400-metre elevation to complete.

While Shimano was trying to fit one incompatible wheel on my bike after another, a Lotto team mechanic rode up through the traffic jam with my spare bike. I have nothing but compliments for his quick thinking in all the confusion. I grabbed my bike and got going as quickly as I could, one minute and twenty-three seconds later. At the start of the day I had been second in classification at eight seconds.

I rode well to make back some time to the lead group, then Hendrik Redant saw that I didn't have a water bottle on the replacement bike, and gave me one for the climb. Later I was

penalised another ten seconds for this. It amounted to a one minute and thirty-three-second loss on a day when I was going to be able to make time on leader Alejandro Valverde and put myself in a winning position. I finished third overall in the 2009 Vuelta a Espana, a bitter one minute and thirty-two seconds down.

A BUNGLED PUNCTURE REPAIR ON STAGE THIRTEEN OF THE 2009 VUELTA A ESPANA CHANGES EVERYTHING.

THE 2009 FLECHE WALLONNE PASSES THROUGH MUR DE HUY.

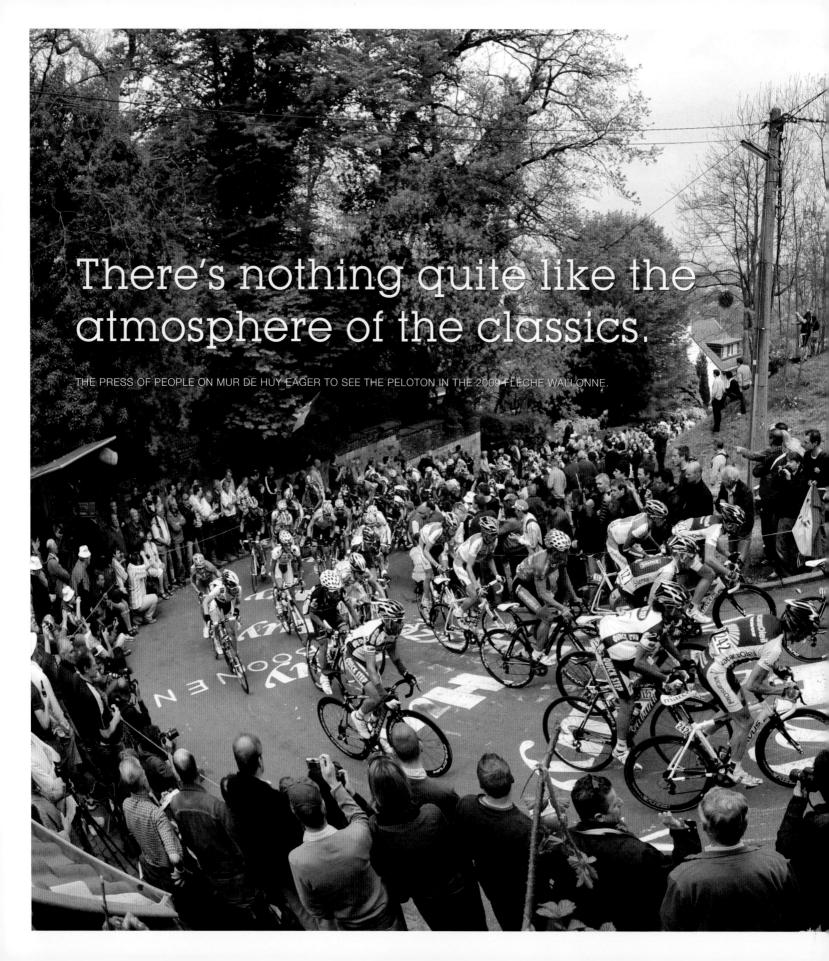

There's nothing quite like the atmosphere of the classics.

THE PRESS OF PEOPLE ON MUR DE HUY EAGER TO SEE THE PELOTON IN THE 2009 FLÈCHE WALLONNE.

Being a 'domestic' or 'worker' for the efforts of the team is something I rarely was in the position to do. My teams normally relied on me for the results and role of 'captain'. Here, in the 2009 Tour de Romandie, I was actually forced to race against my wishes. I had one day of amazing legs here on the way to La Chaux-de-Fonds, riding the entire peloton off teammate Phil Gilbert's wheel. Unfortunately a headwind finish and strong effort by the remainder of the Caisse d'Epargne team brought our little dream team show to an end in the final few kilometres before the finish. Oscar Freire won from a small group finish.

FORCING THE PACE ON STAGE TWO OF THE 2009 TOUR DE ROMANDIE.

BEING TESTED IN the bad conditions of the 2009 Vuelta – the Vuelta comes very late in a long and tiring cycling season and most riders are running well into their reserves of energy and motivation.

ATTACKING ON STAGE FOURTEEN OF THE 2009 VUELTA A ESPANA.

Enjoying a laugh with a slightly less focussed, but more fun, Lance Armstrong on his return to the Tour post-retirement.

READY, WITH LANCE ARMSTRONG, FOR STAGE TWO OF THE 2009 TOUR DE FRANCE.

I GOT A BIT TIRED of being called 'the rider that never attacks'. When I saw that Astana were having a rare moment of difficulty on the uphill start of the stage from Andorra, I jumped into the group that had edged away from the peloton.

On the descent we were caught by Thor Hushovd and Fabian Cancellara, not riders in contention for overall honours, but among the best riders on the planet. Both of them were yelling at me to 'get back to the peloton – you're on GC'.

I stayed just to demonstrate the point of why it's not worth, or possible, for a rider like me to go in early breaks.

GRINDING THROUGH STAGE SEVEN (ABOVE) AND FIFTEEN (LEFT) OF THE 2009 TOUR DE FRANCE.

Some days, racing through the festive crowd, the smell of a BBQ or the sight of those having a champagne picnic on the roadside is enviable.

A PACKED COL DU TOURMALET ON STAGE NINE OF THE 2009 TOUR DE FRANCE.

I like to promote our sport, and sport in general. It's great that because of my results people in Australia who had never watched cycling saw every night of the Tour and loved every minute of it. People are discovering cycling and I'm excited about that.

AUSTRALIAN CYCLISTS POSE ON STAGE TWENTY-ONE OF THE 2009 TOUR DE FRANCE.

IF WE GO BACK to 1994, my first Junior World Championships, when I came second in Vail, and the feeling ... You can't understand the sickening feeling that you have on the podium, when you're standing there in second place and the guy next to you is putting on the rainbow jersey. I've had that often. Always just missing out, and then for it to finally come made that sixteen-year wait worthwhile.

I look back at all those people who beat me – even in my first junior World Championships – and missing out all those times kept me hungry. The more I look back on it as my career has progressed, the happier I am that I didn't win earlier. This is the scenario that has helped keep my hunger for longer.

Really, it's funny to look back on that 2009 season. I'd had so many obstacles to overcome, setbacks that just kept coming through the year – one after another after another. It felt like, for as many weeks as there are in a year, I had setbacks. And there was always Chiara telling me how she saw it: 'One day your honesty will be repaid'.

And, all of a sudden, it was.

ATTACKING IN THE 2009 WORLD ROAD CHAMPIONSHIPS.

ONCE I GOT A GAP, 254 kilometres in to the 2009 World Championships, that remaining six kilometres seemed very, very surreal. To get to wear the rainbow jersey for a year, to win just three kilometers from my home-away-from-home in Stabio, Switzerland. I'd won plenty of time trials and stage races but this was the only World Championships I'd won up to that point, and it was the one that mattered most.

WINNING THE 2009 ELITE MEN'S WORLD ROAD CHAMPIONSHIPS.

As a rider, you put everything on the line to win or lose, and sometimes you win.

RACING OVER THE LINE IN THE 2009 ELITE
MEN'S WORLD ROAD CHAMPIONSHIPS.

PROUDLY PUTTING ON THE RAINBOW JERSEY
AFTER WINNING THE 2009 ELITE MEN'S
WORLD ROAD CHAMPIONSHIPS.

I HAVE COMMITTED more than half of my life to cycling; I've eaten, slept and breathed cycling, and that has got me to where I am today. You have to work at it every step of the way, but that's what is nice about working at cycling: you usually get back what you put into it.

THE 2009 COPPA SABATINI.

2010

Another day at the office
... what a great job!

ONE OF THE PELOTON IN THE 2009 GIRO DI LOMBARDIA.

I'VE ALWAYS JOKED that I learnt to ride up hills quickly so I could start the downhills sooner. It's still the thrill that gets me. When I start a descent, the sensation is still the same. It's what I love about riding my bike: the freedom of flying down the mountain. If you look at the best descenders in the world, they push the boundaries of what's safe and what's not, but it's a considered risk. They're always riding within their limits. It's the same with any high-risk sport: the best ride at a higher threshold. That's why they're at the top of their field. They know what speed they can go through a corner without creating trouble – because of their talent and bike handling.

The ability to stay at the limit is what makes the difference.

TESTING THE LIMIT IN THE 2009
GIRO DI LOMBARDIA.

Some days it's just beautiful.

THIRTY KILOMETRES FROM CADEL'S EUROPEAN BASE IN SWITZERLAND, THE 2009 GIRO DI LOMBARDIA RIDES
BESIDE LAGO COMO IN ARGEGNO, ITALY.

The Tour Down Under 2010 was the starting point
of a key relationship with George Hincapié.

BRINGING IT HOME ON THE 2010 TOUR DOWN UNDER.

With temperatures around
40 degrees and a hilly stage
with a lot of wind, the Tour Down
Under isn't so easy in January.

THE TOUR DOWN UNDER HUGS THE AUSTRALIAN COAST.

DAY FOUR OF THE Tirreno–Adriatico 2010: 235 kilometres in sun and rain and snow through what, on paper, looked to be the toughest stage of the race: up and down all day, passing the earthquake-affected Aquila and finishing on the steep ascents to Chieti. I have to say, the Continental/Easton wheel combo is exceptional in the blindingly wet and cold descents.

Day Five was another long hard day: 216 kilometres of fast racing to the main climb of the day, which reduced the almost 200-strong peloton to just nine riders. Add to that race leader Michele Scarponi crashing and it was quite the drama.

GRINDING THROUGH STAGE SIX OF THE 2010 TIRRENO–ADRIATICO.

POWERING TO WIN THE 2010 FLECHE WALLONNE.

STAGE THREE WAS slightly more hectic than we were hoping for: crashes left, right and centre. I'm not exactly sure why, but between Dutch road furniture, people not paying attention and a very nervous peloton, there were a lot of guys going down. Anyway, they awarded a pink jersey to the best crash avoidance so far, and I got it.

The same chain of events that put me prematurely into pink also took me out of it. A crash at the front of the Sky lead-out train took their race leader, Brad Wiggins, out of the leader's jersey, putting me in it. The next day, another crash by the Sky lead-out train held me up. As you can see here, I was okay stopped behind the crash, until I got taken out from behind seconds after this photo was taken. At least I had some time to be in pink again.

STAGE THREE OF THE 2010 GIRO D'ITALIA

THE MAD CHASE after I picked myself up off the road to get back to the lead group. At this moment, only Cervélo and Carlos Sastre had shared interests in getting back in front, while HTC's Adam Hansen was doing his work at the front for André Greipel, into the headwind. We couldn't close the gap. With a favourable wind blowing from the right side, I tried making seconds anywhere I could in the last kilometres.

Some days the years of
mountain bike experience
become very useful.

WELL DISGUISED, WINNING STAGE SEVEN
OF THE 2010 GIRO D'ITALIA.

The real test of character in cycling ...

AGAINST THE ELEMENTS ON STAGE EIGHT OF THE 2010 GIRO D'ITALIA.

... is getting through the hard days.

SHARING A MOMENT WITH TYLER FARRAR ON STAGE THIRTEEN OF THE 2010 GIRO D'ITALIA.

Zoncolan, Plan de Corones – some of those climbs are just incredible. Everyone told me about Zoncolan, and I found it a bit hard to believe, but when I went and rode it, you feel it in your legs: it's ridiculously hard. I can't say how hard it is. You just don't believe it until you've ridden it. If anyone wants to try a really hard climb, I recommend that; it's not ridiculously steep, but for how long it is, it *is* ridiculously steep.

THE INFAMOUS SULLO ZONCOLAN ON STAGE FIFTEEN OF THE 2010 GIRO D'ITALIA.

I KNOW WHAT my limit is and I'm fully aware when I'm going above and beyond it. I don't know if people believe how hard I'm going. They say, 'Why didn't you just go a bit harder and put in an attack?'

I think, 'Well, I was actually starting to lose vision at that point on the climb ... '

CRESTING STAGE SIXTEEN OF THE 2010 GIRO D'ITALIA.

GETTING DROPPED ON the Mortirolo: recovering from a fever in the first half of the race, on this particular day in the 2010 Giro d'Italia I rode the normal gear ratios for the stage. Just ahead in the distance were my Giro podium chances. This was one of the crucial moments where every bit of physical and mental strength had to be put into the pedals. As I was turning myself insideout to get back to the GC group it was all being captured on TV for viewers' pleasure.

Unfortunately for me, apart from the fact that my suffering was being telecast around the globe, this also meant the team directors of the riders in front of me were probably getting a better idea of my state than I was, allowing them to direct their riders accordingly.

PUSHING THROUGH STAGE NINETEEN OF THE 2010 GIRO D'ITALIA.

A LONG AND WINDING ROAD: THE PELOTON BEGINS TO CLIMB STAGE TWENTY OF THE 2010 GIRO D'ITALIA.

In the really cold weather our brake pads have trouble working and need to warm up; the first corner you get to, you nearly go off the road.

THE PELOTON SPREADS OUT DURING AN ASCENT ON STAGE TWENTY OF THE 2010 GIRO D'ITALIA.

The Giro d'Italia is in May, and you have to remember that if you want to go and see the stages beforehand, most of the mountains are under the snow; you have to go as late as possible.

CAMERAS POISED, A SPARSE FEW WAIT TO SEE THE RIDERS ON STAGE TWENTY OF THE 2010 GIRO D'ITALIA.

The results tell the story.

FACING THE MEDIA DURING THE 2010 GIRO D'ITALIA.

EACH TOUR DE FRANCE gives you a good base to work
from and improve on, for everyone, from myself to the
mechanics, the soigneurs, the directors – everyone.
Every year you learn more. You learn more about
yourself; you learn more about your competitors; you
learn more about your sport. Each year I hope that
with that one more year of experience I'm going to get
better, I'm going to do better, and therefore I'm going
to perform better. With two years at less than a minute
from winning the Tour, I feel like I'm getting closer
and closer to winning.

I don't lament lost races. What's the point? Second is
a place. It's what it is.

A FAMILIAR SCENE ON THE HOT AND DRY 2010 TOUR DE FRANCE:
FABIAN CANCELLARA IN YELLOW.

ONLOOKERS CREATE THE ATMOSPHERE ON COL DU TOURMALET DURING THE 2010 TOUR DE FRANCE.

WHILE EVERYONE HAS a difficult job – race organisers, sponsors, police – when the conditions are really unusual or the roads are dangerous, in the end it's the cyclists who risk an injury or worse.

The stage started with a perfectly flat, straight road, no bumps, no obstacles, nothing. I was thinking, 'This is a good time to relax a little bit and save some energy for later'. Unfortunately, it seems quite a few riders in the peloton were relaxing at the same time, and, coming into a left-hand turn, I didn't even see some riders rolling on the road in front of me. I ran straight into them before I could slow down and landed really hard on my left side, taking most of the impact on my elbow and wrist.

Still riding with a broken elbow was actually quite enjoyable: I was able to appreciate being in the Tour, feeling the atmosphere, being encouraged in almost every accent imaginable, as opposed to the usual performance-based concentration (and stress) I'm used to feeling in July.

But the cobbles on the Champs-Élysées in Paris sure hurt when you have a broken elbow.

WEARING KINESIO TAPES ON HIS ARM IN STAGE NINE OF THE 2010 TOUR DE FRANCE.

2011

The team do everything they can and that's all I ask of them.

THE TEAM TAKES ON THE 2011 TIRRENO–ADRIATICO, AND CADEL GIVES IT HIS ALL.

IF YOU DO a couple of simple adjustments on, for example, the wheels on your bike, you can get a quarter of a second a kilometre, or, by doing something else, one second a kilometre better. And that might make the difference that means winning the Tour de France by ten seconds. So of course you want the best set of wheels you can get. In 110 kilometres of time trialling if I'd got one quarter of a second per kilometre better, it would have been all the difference I needed.

You can always feel what's good and what's bad when you try a new bike, but I always like to quantify it. Sometimes you do the tests and it isn't actually any faster than the bike you have. Or maybe you stick with what you have because it handles much better and is much safer. You might save a quarter of a second per kilometre, but if you crash and don't even finish the stage, well, that isn't going to win the race.

IN PERPETUAL TRAINING AND TESTING WITH COACH ANDREA MORELLI.

If you can make your hobby your profession, you never have to work another day in your life.

CHIARA SETS THE PACE.

When you have success it breeds motivation, confidence, everything. I just rode more and more because I could, for a start, but also because I liked it. I got better and better so I rode more and more. As much time as I had, I rode. Any spare time was spent on the bike. That's all my training was. I didn't mean to be a bike rider; it was like, 'Oh, this is good; I like this. You can make a profession out of this?!' And from that point onwards I wanted to be a bike rider.

LEADING THE PELOTON ON STAGE FIVE OF THE 2011 TOUR DE ROMANDIE.

Every day the team delivered me to where I really needed to be, and that left me fresh and ready to finish off the job.

WINNING STAGE FOUR OF THE 2011 TOUR DE FRANCE, AND THE FINISH WITH ALBERTO CONTADOR (LEFT).

EVERY SO OFTEN you can look and see how they're going,
but often looks can be deceiving. Contador is getting better.
Certainly I was always prepared for anything – you've got
to be prepared for anything in this sport – but I wasn't really
counting on him attacking in the Col de Manse. It's not a steep
climb, it's not one that really suits him, and it's quite a way
from the finish, but he went there. If I were in his shoes, I'd be
trying anything because he's got everything to gain.

ATTACKING ON STAGE SIXTEEN OF THE 2011 TOUR DE FRANCE

Initially the defensive effort on Col Galibier was made to *not lose* the Tour, but it became the key effort to win the 2011 Tour de France.

CHASING ON STAGE EIGHTEEN OF THE 2011 TOUR DE FRANCE.

The fight on Alpe d'Huez became a battle of
mental strength rather than leg strength.

GRIMACING THROUGH STAGE NINETEEN OF THE 2011 TOUR DE FRANCE.

Time trialing to victory in the Tour – twenty years after Indurain, without realising it, I had repeated his method of success to win cycling's ultimate prize … the Credit Lyonnais Lion!

WINNING STAGE TWENTY (LEFT), AND TAKING THE TOP STEP ON THE PODIUM OF THE 2011 TOUR DE FRANCE.

A major part of Lance Armstrong's success in the Tour de France was his strong team. Our success was thanks to a strong team bond.

TO BE THERE wearing the yellow jersey – for my team, my country, for the group of people around me
– it left me a little lost for words. It's going to take me a little time to realise what's happened. It's twenty
years of working hard and coming close a couple of times. But better late than never! For two years I
was really unlucky, coming so close to winning, but maybe that's just made it all the more special now.

FINALLY WINNING THE TOUR DE FRANCE.

MIGUEL INDURAIN

TONY ROMINGER

GIANNI BUGNO

Influences

I'VE BEEN INSPIRED by great riders such as Miguel Indurain and Tony Rominger. As a young Tour de France fan watching the seemingly invincible 'Big Mig' win yet another Tour, I'd always known about Tony, but later he would become a large part of my life.

The first time I ever saw him was when he was invited out to Australia to ride the Melbourne to Mount Buller one-day race. It just happened to start a few kilometres from my high school. Of course, I took the opportunity to go and see him as he was then one of the best riders in the world. Years later, we met again when Tony went into retirement and became a rider manager.

When he started his own management company in 2004, I was honoured that he asked me to join his clientele. Over the years since, we have built both a professional relationship and a personal one. Tony works in the world of cycling, likes good wine ... we have some similarities! Most

of all, though, it's been great having a man of his experience and know-how have faith in me during the bad times, and, ultimately, become part of my 'core' team of important and trusted individuals.

After winning the Worlds in Mendrisio, Tony asked if he could have a jersey for his office; it was only then that I realised what I had done that day.

Then there's Gianni Bugno: his character as a rider was one thing, but it was his character off the bike combined with his riding abilities that impressed me, and made him a real 'champion' in my mind. His gentle manner and modesty, combined with incredible strength and versatility as a rider, impressed me from an early age. How could you win a world title and only hold up one hand in victory?

Years later, without realising it, I did exactly that. The man who I share a birthday with is still someone I have great admiration for.

From Chiara

A FEW YEARS AGO, someone taught me how to see the good side of things and use it to improve my life. With that idea always in mind, I continued my journey with Cadel through the unbelievable surprises that life gives us every day. Before that, I didn't know how to be patient; I didn't know how to listen. I didn't know that tiny details were parts of a perfect painting, and I didn't know that you have to find your own way to happiness.

How do people imagine our life 'behind the scenes'? For every minute when you see Cadel racing, there's been a long period of training, through sunshine, rain, wind and even snow. There's travel – a lot of travel – which means suitcases, packing and unpacking. And there's sacrifice: Cadel gives up time for friends, for family, for himself. Being under constant scrutiny, answering the requests from the media, bring added pressure. For me, there's the rush of adrenaline when Cadel wins a race and I feel like we've both won it, or when he walks out of the airport, finally coming home. But then there's making him sit for a while to sign documents and do paperwork when I know he's dead tired.

Life with Cadel is a rollercoaster of emotions and adventures: we never know what will happen tomorrow. When I'm not with him, I miss him, but I know he's off doing what he loves to do: riding his bike. I hope he'll keep on doing that for the rest of his life.

Of course, you need a bit of luck along the way, but my best can often be good enough to be one of the best in the world. I'll continue to do anything I can to achieve that. For as long as Chiara will let me race professionally as a bike rider, I've got the motivation to do it.

Achievements

1994

2nd   World Championships (junior), Cross Country (MTB), Vail, USA

1995

3rd   World Championships (junior), Cross Country (MTB), Kirchzarten, Germany

3rd   World Championships (junior), Time Trial (road), Forli, Italy

1996

5th   World Cup (elite), Cross Country (MTB), Cairns, Australia

3rd   World Championships (Under 23), Cross Country (MTB), Cairns, Australia

9th   Olympics, Cross Country (MTB), Atlanta, USA

1997

1st   World Cup, Cross Country (MTB), Wellington, New Zealand

2nd   World Cup, Cross Country (MTB), St-Wendel, Germany

2nd   World Cup, Cross Country (MTB), Budapest, Hungary

1st   World Cup, Cross Country (MTB), Vail, USA

3rd   World Cup (elite), Cross Country (MTB), Overall Results

2nd   World Championships (Under 23), Cross Country (MTB), Château-d'Oex, Switzerland

1998

1st   Mount Buller Classic (road), Mt Buller, Australia

2nd   Stage 2, Geelong Bay Classic Series (road), Portarlington, Australia

2nd   General Classification, Redlands Bicycle Classic (road), California, USA

1st   World Cup, Cross Country (MTB), Silves, Portugal

2nd   World Cup, Cross Country (MTB), St-Wendel, Germany

1st   World Cup (elite), Cross Country (MTB), Plymouth, UK

1st   World Cup, Cross Country (MTB), Canmore, Canada

3rd   World Cup, Cross Country (MTB), Bromont, Canada

1st   World Cup (elite), Cross Country (MTB), Overall Results

1999

2nd   Stage 2, Mount Buller Cup (road), Mt Buller, Australia

2nd   Prologue, Tour of Tasmania (road), Launceston, Australia

1st   Stage 3, Tour of Tasmania (road), Mt Wellington, Australia

1st   General Classification, Tour of Tasmania (road), Australia

2nd   World Cup, Cross Country (MTB), Napa Valley, USA

2nd   World Cup, Cross Country (MTB), Sydney, Australia

1st   World Cup, Cross Country (MTB), Madrid, Spain

2nd   World Cup, Cross Country (MTB), Big Bear, USA

2nd   World Cup, Cross Country (MTB), Canmore, Canada

3rd   World Cup, Cross Country (MTB), Houffalize, Belgium

1st   World Cup (elite), Cross Country (MTB), Overall Results

2nd   World Championships (Under 23), Cross Country (MTB), Åre, Sweden

2000

3rd   Australian National Championships (elite), Cross Country (MTB), Kooralbyn, Australia

1st   World Cup, Cross Country (MTB), Mont Sainte-Anne, Canada

1st   World Cup, Cross Country (MTB), Canmore, Canada

3rd   World Cup, Cross Country (MTB), Swansea, USA

7th   Olympics, Cross Country (MTB), Sydney, Australia

2001

3rd   World Cup, Cross Country (MTB), Grouse Mountain, Canada

2nd   World Cup, Cross Country (MTB), Kaprun, Austria

1st   A Travers Lausanne (road), Lausanne, Switzerland

1st   Stage 4, Österreich Rundfahrt (road), Kitzbüheler Horn, Austria

1st   General Classification, Österreich Rundfahrt (road), Austria

2nd   Stage 2, Brixia Tour (road), Lumezzane, Italy

1st   General Classification, Brixia Tour (road), Italy

2nd   Japan Cup (road), Japan

2002

1st   Stage 5, Tour Down Under (road), Tanunda, Australia

2nd   Stage 6, Paris–Nice (road), Col d'Eze, France

3rd   General Classification, Settimana Ciclistica Internazionale Coppi-Bartali (road), Italy

3rd   General Classification, Tour de Romandie (road), Switzerland

2nd   Stage 13, Giro d'Italia (road), San Giacomo, Italy

3rd   Stage 14, Giro d'Italia (road), Numana, Italy

1st   Stage 4, Uniqa Classic (road), Grossmaning, Austria

1st   Commonwealth Games, Time Trial (road), Manchester, UK

2nd   Commonwealth Games (road), Manchester, UK

3rd   Rominger Classic (road), Engelberg, Switzerland

2004

3rd   Stage 4, Vuelta Ciclista a Murcia (road), Alto Collado Bermejo, Spain

3rd   General Classification, Vuelta Ciclista a Murcia (road), Spain

1st   Stage 2, Österreich Rundfahrt (road), Kitzbüheler Horn, Austria

1st   General Classification, Österreich Rundfahrt (road), Austria

2005

2nd   Stage 5, Paris–Nice (road), Toulon, France

4th   Stage 16, Tour de France (road), Pau, France

1st   Stage 7, Deutschland Tour (road), Feldberg, Germany

2nd   Mountains Classification, Deutschland Tour (road), Germany

2006

3rd   Stage 3, Tour Down Under (road), Yankalilla, Australia

3rd   Stage 3, Tour de Romandie (road), Leysin, Switzerland

3rd   Stage 4, Tour de Romandie (road), Sion, Switzerland

1st   Stage 5, Tour de Romandie (road), Lausanne, Switzerland

1st   General Classification, Tour de Romandie (road), Switzerland

2nd   Points Classification, Tour de Romandie (road), Switzerland

3rd   Stage 8, Tour de Suisse (road), Ambri, Switzerland

2nd   Stage 9, Tour de Suisse (road), Bern, Switzerland

4th   Stage 11, Tour de France (road), Val d'Aran–Pla-de-Beret, France

4th   Stage 16, Tour de France (road), La Toussuire, France

5th   General Classification, Tour de France (road), France

3rd   Stage 6, Tour de Pologne (road), Karpacz, Poland

3rd   Stage 7, Tour de Pologne (road), Karpacz, Poland

2nd   General Classification, Tour de Pologne (road), Poland

2007

1st Stage 1, Part b, Settimana Ciclistica Internazionale Coppi-Bartali (road), Misano Adriatico, Italy

3rd Stage 7, Critérium du Dauphiné Libéré (road), Annecy, France

2nd General Classification, Critérium du Dauphiné Libéré (road), France

3rd Points Classification, Critérium du Dauphiné Libéré (road), France

3rd Stage 9, Tour de France (road), Briançon, France

1st Stage 13, Tour de France (road), Albi, France

4th Stage 16, Tour de France (road), Gourette–Col d'Aubisque, France

2nd Stage 19, Tour de France (road), Angoulême, France

2nd General Classification, Tour de France (road), France

3rd Wiesbauer Rathauskriterium (road), Austria

1st Castillon-la-Bataille (road), France

2nd Marcoles (road), France

3rd Gouden Pijl Emmen (road), Netherlands

1st Stage 2, Test Event Beijing 2008 (road), Beijing, China

2nd Stage 10, Vuelta a España (road), Andorra (Vallnord/sector Arcalís), Spain

2nd Stage 18, Vuelta a España (road), Avila, Spain

4th General Classification, Vuelta a España (road), Spain

1st General Classification, UCI ProTour (road)

2008

1st Stage 2, Vuelta a Andalucia (Ruta del Sol) (road), La Zubia, Spain

3rd General Classification, Vuelta a Andalucia (Ruta del Sol) (road), Spain

1st Stage 4, Paris–Nice (road), Station du Mont Serein–Mont Ventoux, France

1st Stage 3, Settimana Ciclistica Internazionale Coppi-Bartali (road), Pavullo, Italy

1st General Classification, Settimana Ciclistica Internazionale Coppi-Bartali (road), Italy

2nd Stage 6, Vuelta Ciclista al País Vasco (road), Orio, Spain

2nd General Classification, Vuelta Ciclista al País Vasco (road), Spain

2nd Waalse Pijl (road), Huy, Belgium

3rd Stage 3, Critérium du Dauphiné Libéré (road), Saint-Paul-en-Jarez, France

2nd Stage 5, Critérium du Dauphiné Libéré (road), Morzine, France

2nd General Classification, Critérium du Dauphiné Libéré (road), France

3rd Points Classification, Critérium du Dauphiné Libéré (road), France

4th Stage 4, Tour de France (road), Cholet, France

3rd Stage 6, Tour de France (road), Super-Besse, France

2nd General Classification, Tour de France (road), France

2nd Bavikhove (road), Belgium

2009

3rd   Stage 3, Vuelta a Andalucia (Ruta del Sol) (road), Benahavis, Spain

4th   Stage 6, Paris–Nice (road), La Montagne de Lure, France

4th   Stage 2, Settimana Ciclistica Internazionale Coppi-Bartali (road), Faenza, Italy

2nd   Stage 3, Settimana Ciclistica Internazionale Coppi-Bartali (road), Serramazzoni, Italy

1st   Stage 5, Settimana Ciclistica Internazionale Coppi-Bartali (road), Sassuolo, Italy

2nd   General Classification, Settimana Ciclistica Internazionale Coppi-Bartali (road), Italy

2nd   Stage 3, Vuelta Ciclista al País Vasco (road), Eibar, Spain

4th   General Classification, Vuelta Ciclista al País Vasco (road), Spain

5th   Waalse Pijl (road), Huy, Belgium

1st   Stage 1, Critérium du Dauphiné Libéré (road), Nancy, France

2nd   Stage 4, Critérium du Dauphiné Libéré (road), Valence, France

3rd   Stage 7, Critérium du Dauphiné Libéré (road), Saint-François-Longchamp, France

2nd   General Classification, Critérium du Dauphiné Libéré (road), France

1st   Points Classification, Critérium du Dauphiné Libéré (road), France

5th   Stage 1, Tour de France (road), Monaco, France

4th   Stage 8, Vuelta a España (road), Alto de Aitana, Spain

3rd   Stage 19, Vuelta a España (road), La Granja. Real Fábrica de Cristales, Spain

3rd   Stage 20, Vuelta a España (road), Toledo, Spain

3rd   General Classification, Vuelta a España (road), Spain

1st   World Championships (elite), (road), Mendrisio, Switzerland

2010

3rd   Grand Prix de Wallonie (road), Belgium

Most Aggressive Rider
   Stage 5, Tour Down Under (road), Willunga, Australia

6th   General Classification, Tour Down Under (road), Australia

3rd   Stage 6, Tirreno Adriatico (road), Macerata, Italy

3rd   General Classification, Tirenno–Adriatico (road), Italy

1st   La Flèche Wallonne (road), Belgium

5th   Liege-Bastogne-Liege (road), Belgium

1st   Stage 7, Giro d'Italia (road), Montalcino, Italy

5th   General Classification, Giro d'Italia (road), Italy

1st   Points Classification, Giro d'Italia (road), Italy

4th   Mountains Classification, Giro d'Italia (road), Italy

2011

1st   Stage 6, Tirreno–Adriatico (road), Macerata, Italy

1st   General Classification, Tirreno–Adriatico (road), Italy

2nd   Stage 2, Tour de Romandie (road), Romont, Switzerland

1st   General Classification, Tour de Romandie (road), Switzerland

2nd   General Classification, Criterium du Dauphiné Libéré (road), France

1st   Stage 4, Tour de France (road), Mûr-de-Bretagne, France

1st   General Classification, Tour de France (road) France

4th   Points Classification, Tour de France (road), France

4th   King of the Mountain Classification, Tour de France (road), France

IN MEMORIAM, ALDO SASSI (PHOTO BY RICHARD BAYBUTT).

Acknowledgements

WHAT STARTED OUT as an idea in conversation over dinner with Australian sport journalist Rupert Guinness is now a finished product.

Thanks to Graham for his passion for the sport and his ability as a photographer to capture the crucial moments of our sport and present them to the world. Thanks also to photographers Mal Fearon, Tom Moran and Richard Baybutt.

To everyone who believed in my career – starting back in 1992 with Damian Grundy, who taught me to be a professional and work hard in sport all through my mountain bike career, and continuing with Aldo Sassi, since our first meeting in 2001, who always had faith in me and often had more confidence in my own abilities than I did.

Thanks to everyone who always believed in me and in true sport.